Ice Cream
On Thursdays

Ice Cream On Thursdays

Jeanette Voyzey

To order additional copies of this book, contact:
Xlibris LLC
0-800-056-3182
www.xlibrispublishing.co.uk
Orders@xlibrispublishing.co.uk
522178

We are all given a bowl of ingredients to stir—it is our life. What we do with this is down to us. We have choices to make, places to go, highways to travel, crossroads to navigate, all of which makes us the individuals we become. There are third-party influencers; however, to whom we choose to listen is for us to decide. We are responsible for our own destiny. We may have guidance from those who think they know better (maybe they do). However, is it better for them or better for us?

It is worth remembering that oysters turn their little irritations into pearls. This quote attributed to American poet and philosopher Ralph Waldo Emerson (1803-1882) sums all this up perfectly: 'Do not go where the path may lead, go instead where there is no path and leave a trail.'

I would like to dedicate this book to my three daughters, my grandson and two granddaughters.
And Dr Thomas Barnardo.

PREFACE

I have written the following to try to make some sense of the endless letters and notes on my early life, which I obtained from Barnardo's. There have been stories written by others who grew up in childrens' homes which I have read with some understanding. My records from Barnardo's, covering my life from losing my mother to meeting my future husband, were archived, and therefore, some of the print is hard to read. The one emotion I felt during my life was defiance; however, until I was old enough to know the meaning of the word, I couldn't label it. Everything written in my records is, of course, pertinent to my life. I had hoped that if I am lucky enough to find a publisher, I could include copies of some of these letters. However as they were printed from microfilm they are not clear enough to reproduce. We all have a story to tell, and I hope this will be of use, historically speaking, to future generations of my family.

This is not a 'woe is me' tale; it is a simple description of survival against the odds. Many people worked behind the scenes to enable me to be cared for; however, a lot was missed by them. It seemed to me, reading the endless letters between the authorities, they did their best with what they had. Remember, this was the 1940s/1950s. I was one of the fortunate ones. I did go off the rails a couple of times, and I wasn't the easiest child. However, in my defence, I was reacting to the circumstances in which I found myself. The biggest problem was that once I started fighting (which was what I felt I had to do), when life did become easier, I didn't recognize it. I made many mistakes, and at times I found it hard to respond to kindness. However, I have written just a potted history of my life and times growing up, and although I could maybe have said a lot more, I feel that embellishing and overdescription are not necessary.

As I grew older, I became more and more confused, but at the same time I wanted to give rather than receive. I suppose, at a young age, I thought everyone struggled as I had. I wasn't worldly wise even though I thought I knew it all. That is the one thing I had in common with most young people. I never lost the defiance and fighting spirit. I still have it to this day, some fifty-five years later. I don't think I acquired the humility which I see in a few people today. Sometimes it is a help, sometimes a hindrance. Outwardly, I have the 'glass half full' and optimistic nature. This belies the struggle underneath for emotional security. I find it hard to relate to people's insecurities and do not suffer fools gladly. However, at odds with myself, I do have empathy for my fellow human beings and would always be there for anyone in trouble. Some people complain about having elderly parents to care for at a time when they want to do things for themselves. I just say, 'Thank your lucky stars you still have your mother or father or both, value them.' As the saying goes, 'If you have a mother, cherish her with care. You will never know how much you need her till you see her empty chair.'

CHAPTER ONE

I gazed at the door in front of me, shiny black paint. This time it held no terrors. Uncertainty, yes, as to what lay on the other side, but no distress or tears. There was just the ground floor available to see. As it stood, this place was so different to the reality all those years ago. How could I put into words what this house had meant to me? It was my home, my stability in an ever-changing world. Cambridge Cottage was one of the few remaining houses left at the children's Village Home. I had been given an invite to attend Barnardo's centenary celebrations and was hoping to maybe meet up with some people who shared my time here. I was asked if I would like to write my name against the cottage I occupied, and I scanned the list already there, eagle-eyed, hoping to recognize someone. Unfortunately, there wasn't one name I knew.

Somehow being back seemed poignant and unreal, which was at odds with the happy times I spent here. Did I want to view the only cottage open to the public? I wasn't too sure; however, here I was, not sorry because I could think of Matron, the comfortable kitchen and the warmth, my attempts at baking, and the general affection shown to me and the other children who shared this home. I was the eldest at ten years old. It was coincidental that this one open cottage now in museum form was my home for three years. And until I grew up and married, it was where I spent the best years of my life.

The majority of the Village had disappeared; the land was used for building houses and a supermarket. However, the reception area was still there along with the church. How pretty it looked. The timber-framed cottages now used for other purposes were home to lots of girls and boys from all backgrounds and age groups. Also, Dr Barnardo's final resting place is in the grounds with an ornate memorial gravestone. The church was where, I have to say, I saw a great deal of Sunday morning service, afternoon Sunday school, and evensong (well, I suppose it kept me out of mischief for one day at least). This is me saying this as an adult. I felt differently as a child as a small reference later will tell you.

A group of actors were playing out the life story of Dr Barnardo. What a wonderful person, and where would I and many others be without him? Dr Barnardo was born in July 1845 in Dublin to John Michaelis Barnardo (a furrier) and his second wife, Abigail, a member of the Plymouth Brethren. Sadly, he died at the age of just sixty in September 1905.

I mentioned distress and tears. I was in this very spot many years ago, with only the clothes I had on, and a carrier bag holding a few personal possessions. My aunt who had cared for me was no longer able to do so due to ill health and a miserable husband. I cried, yes. I cried a lot. I was frightened and upset at what lay ahead. Somehow I remember being taken in, shown my bedroom (which I would share), the bathroom, and the dining room. We also had a locker each for our personal possessions. None of this meant too much at the time because I felt distraught at such a huge change in my life yet again. I was born in Eastleigh in Hampshire to a family of dissenters, not in the sense of church doctrine, but more on not believing at all. Except my mother, of course. Tempers flared at every corner. I remember a fully laden dining table being overturned at meal times, sometimes completely out of the blue.

My mother suffered at the hands of a philandering husband and coped with ill health. Winifred Violet Jackson-Smith died on 26th February 1951 at the age of forty-six years from gallstones. I feel so sad for her. How did she cope? I last saw her in a hospital side room, beckoning me in, and I ran away. To this day I regret not going into her outstretched arms. I want to say, 'Sorry Mum.' I want to say, 'I know that you suffered and how you cared for me and ignored your sickness and sadness for my sake.'

I had no idea at the age of just six years that I was a bouncing ball between a father denying paternity, the National Society for the Prevention of Cruelty to Children (NSPCC), Barnardo's, and the courts. My so-called father refused to take any interest in me. He begged and pleaded to the NSPCC and Barnardo's to take me off his hands! When he had explored all avenues and had nowhere else to go, he took me to the street and sat me on the kerb in the gutter with a note pinned to my clothes asking—no, *demanding*—that someone take me in.

A kind lady came to me and said she was making me a winter coat (at least someone was aware of my plight) and needed me to try it on. She dressed me in an itchy navy-blue coat, which was still full of pins and was prickly. How do you feel grateful at six years old? You don't, and I remember complaining bitterly to her as one pin after another stuck in me. This was the start of a new chapter. My father? Nowhere to be seen! This lady, Mrs Simmons, led me by the hand to a neighbour who agreed to give me a home.

I must point out that I have a sister, ten years older, and a brother, fifteen years older (they were responsible for the table incidents). They disappeared into the armed services. How did I come to be here? Well, it seems having left my mother for other women this poor excuse for a man visited her on the odd occasion, and I was the result. This was never proven (although he did allow his name to be put on my birth certificate). By the time I found out for certain that he'd denied paternity, he was dead. The writing was on the wall as I was to find out much later. Even then, the two people whom I thought were my brother and sister had been told I wasn't their true sibling.

So my life with the family who took me in began. My memory of this time is not very clear, except to say that Mr Roberts worked with my so-called father as a cable layer and had the same missing fingers—a consequence of the job, I have since realized. I presume I was well cared for, and as all kids did at that time, we played in the street until dark. I had food and a warm bed and the very itchy unlined wool coat.

The man whom I thought was my father was called George, so I will refer to him as just that from now on. I feel it is okay to use his name as neither he nor any family survives.

I don't really know what went on behind the scenes, but suffice it to say, George and his woman friend turned up one day at the house where I was staying, asking if I would like to go and live with them. Well, this woman (Gladys) had been in our house to cook for us after my mother died and before I was ceremoniously disposed of, and all I remembered about her were burnt custard and the smell of an awful perfume. I was grabbed by the shoulders and more or less forced to agree to go, but I won and wouldn't budge. What brought about this change of heart by George? It was money. He didn't want to pay a penny for me, and he pleaded poverty even though by now he was living in a very nice house in the best part of town with a wealthy woman who couldn't cook custard. I was then informed by the family who took me in that I would have to go as I was rude, insolent, and expensive to keep! Not too bad for a seven-year-old then. The fighting spirit had begun! I thought at the time, 'Do you really mean me?' However, as time went on, I began to think they were right! I shared a room with their elder daughter who had the annoying habit of swaying backwards and forwards in bed to get herself to sleep. The creaking springs kept me awake for hours. For some reason this bothered me. I couldn't say why, but it seemed worrying and very odd at the time.

I don't remember much about my early school days. I think we played with beads and painted pictures, and from what I recall, there wasn't a lot of actual learning. When my mother died, a teacher, a kindly lady called Mrs Patterson, gave me two shillings and sixpence, or a half-crown (as it was known then), which I promptly lost on the way home. It rolled into someone's garden. I went in to find it and was thrown out and told by the owner that if they found it, it was theirs. I had no idea of the value of money, so I just shrugged my shoulders and walked off. Little did I know then that most of my childhood and teenage years were about how much I was costing in monetary terms.

I went straight to where I called home and didn't mention the money. Toffee apples upside down on a plank of greased wood nailed to the gatepost were for sale at two pence. Wow, they looked good. They wouldn't miss one; only they did! And I had the bruises to prove it after the beating I got for stealing. This paved the way for more violence. The family didn't want me any more. I had become a liability, like a bad smell they couldn't get rid of. My legs were red, raw, and very sore through playing outside in the dark, getting wet, and not drying them properly. I skipped, played hopscotch (chalked on the pavement), and generally amused myself.

I had nothing to call my own and had sat on the pavement and watched George clear out our house, giving what few toys I had to an illegitimate son just a year or two older than me, although what he was going to do with a china doll that cried and moved her eyelids was anyone's guess. Then he hugged my toy monkey, which I had won in a baby contest my mother had entered me in. Once more desolation and loneliness were the order of the day, although then I couldn't put names to my emotions. I just remember crying and shouting, 'They are mine,' my cries falling on deaf ears. The one thing which is firmly entrenched in my memory is the emptiness I felt. How could someone take away those childhood memories and not feel something? George managed it.

Strange to say, I had a maternal grandmother living just around the corner. I say strange because at the time I didn't know why I wasn't living with her. However, it all came to light later on. I remember spending a lot of time with her whilst my mother was still alive. She would collect me from school and give me a penny to spend in the sweet shop on the way home; then we would go to her house for tea and play games and listen to *Mrs Dale's Diary* on the radio. We would use a toasting fork to toast bread by the fire and spread it with Marmite. I had the feeling my mother must have been quite ill for most of my life. I don't remember her taking or collecting me from school, which I am sure she would have done had she been able. However, when she died, I saw very little of my grandmother. I assume now she was grieving for her daughter. There is a short reference to her in my records that she couldn't take me in because she lived in a retirement bungalow that didn't allow resident children. Also, she only had one bedroom.

Even though very young, I was aware of the wonderful handmade furniture my grandmother had. It seemed so different to anything I had seen before. There were the plain dark tables, chairs, etc. These were, as I was to learn later, classed as post-war utility. I found out much later hers were made by, I think, her brother or at least a family member. I remember loving her very much. Her cottage-style garden was full of blackcurrants, redcurrants, and plums, which I was allowed to pick. She was a very smartly dressed lady. What she felt about George was never documented. Her clothes and handmade furniture were at odds with the newspaper squares tied up with string to use as toilet paper in her outside loo.

In the background to all this, George was still trying to get rid of me. To this day his letters still make me cry, saying how upset he was that no one took any notice of his pleas for someone to take me off his hands. What a cruel individual he must have been.

It seems, as I put this all into words, quite a contradiction, him saying I could live with him and his woman but at the same time trying to find someone to take me off his hands. I suppose he didn't have a choice. His pleading and 'poor me' attitude hadn't worked, so was he trying to save face with the family who took me in? I don't know if that would even bother him. This is a part of my life of which I have no understanding, being so young.

How did my mother—a tall, attractive, intelligent, and articulate lady—end up with someone like George? (In spite of being very young, I remember her so well.) I will never know the answer. It is and will always remain a mystery to me. If I could have her back, it would be the one question I would ask. Somehow her background was so different to how she ended up. I suppose George must have charmed his way into her life. Who knows?

CHAPTER TWO

In 1952 I was taken by George to his sister, with nothing but the clothes I had on. I don't think I would have had much to take as he had given all my toys to his son. He had managed to persuade Isabel (of whom I knew nothing) to look after me. Aunt Isabel, so another strange place to adjust to. Why did everyone seem so old? Did she really want me? Probably not at the time. George was very persuasive. This was very much a carrot-and-stick time for me. My aunt was obviously very fond of me, but she was also very cruel. The one thing I didn't know was that the NSPCC was monitoring my life, doing very little, just watching and waiting and writing spurious letters and notes to each other. Barnardo's had at this stage refused to take me in because I wasn't an orphan and had family (of sorts) to care for me. Several letters passed between my aunt Isabel, the NSPCC, and George at the time. These mostly contained complaints about George and his refusal to pay any keep for me. He managed £1 a week, but it wasn't enough. Isabel's husband was a miserable, dour man who constantly complained about the fact that I was there and how much it cost to keep me. He nagged my aunt to send me packing, but she said she couldn't as she had become fond of me. Unsurprisingly, I wasn't adapting too well to another change in my short life. I played in the street, had a couple of friends, and earned money—a shiny sixpence—shelling peas or beans for the neighbours. (There was no pre-packed supermarket food all those years ago.) My uncle would come out to the street, yelling at us for making too much noise. Apart from that, he never spoke to me. He was rooted to his stool in the kitchen, where he would watch Isabel do everything, feigning ill health. He did, however, have a healthy pair of lungs on him when he chose to come to the street. I shared a room with my ninety-year-old paternal grandmother, who was bedridden. I remember trying to entertain her, making her laugh sometimes with my antics. We seemed to build up some kind of rapport, although I don't remember being that close to her. She would ask me to read to her, which I did. I wondered what she did for company before I came as no one came to see her, just the nurses to wash and feed her.

I was hardly ever allowed friends indoors because my aunt had a bed and breakfast for actors working in the local theatre. They meant nothing to me at the time; however, our most famous house guests were Winifred Atwell and Arthur Lucan (Old Mother Riley) and also Mary Martin (Larry Hagman's mother) stayed whilst performing in Oklahoma. None of my friends were aware or knew of these people, so I don't know why they were banned from the house. On the odd occasion when they were allowed inside, they had to sit on the stairs to wait for me. Celebrities didn't have the status they have now. They were just considered to be people who happened to be in the acting profession making a living like the rest of the adults of the time. In fact, I don't think they were labelled 'celebrities'.

I would walk to school and call for friends on the way. I got some comfort from the homely smells emanating from some of houses, and I wished I had that kind of haven to come home to. I admit to feeling jealous of the fact that my friends had parents to care for them. In fact, this is the only time envy has crept into my life.

I mentioned carrot and stick. Sometimes my aunt was very caring; other times she would lock me in the outside toilet out of the way for what seemed like hours at a time. She would also beat me with a wooden coat hanger. I had bruises again, which were not noticed by anyone at school or anywhere for that matter. I suppose I was naughty, but I don't remember doing anything too bad. The carrot side saw me become an ice skater. Isabel bought me my own boots and made my outfits. The stick side saw me grounded because I mentioned a strange man who would follow me home from the ice rink, sometimes in the dark. It was said I had encouraged this person, apart from the fact that I wouldn't know how to. I didn't speak to him. I was very scared. The odd thing was this man would send me presents. Having followed me home, he knew where I lived, and I got boxes of handkerchiefs elaborately embroidered once or twice. I don't know what was done about this, but suffice it to say, we never saw him again.

Even though my aunt spoiled me with ice-skating lessons, a beautiful doll's pram, and dollies (I had to have one white doll and one black doll; I have no idea why), we went from day to day with what was for me, I suppose, somewhat bordering on a normal life. On Sunday evenings we would go on short coach trips, usually called mystery tours. Well, the mystery to me was that, as these were local forays into New Forest, they were not much of a mystery. Sorry! I said I was a difficult child! The best time was a holiday to Ireland; however, the worse time was getting there! A train to Holyhead, which took forever, and a trip across the Irish Sea on a cattle boat. I had seen the cows loaded before the passengers, then heard them lowing all the way over. The sea was rough. I was sick, and at that time, I hated the world and everyone in it and my aunt and uncle, in particular. We arrived in Dun Laoghaire with me moaning and sulking. This didn't last too long, however. Most vehicles in Dublin were horse-drawn, including the taxis. This was fun and so exciting, and I was back to my usual sunny nature. However, more grist to the mill for uncle. 'That child goes when we get back!'

We stayed in a Bed & Breakfast in Dublin with a lovely, jolly landlady who, for some reason, took a shine to me and took me to see her cat with her newly born kittens, which quite naturally I wanted and didn't shut up about for a while. A clip around the ear from Isabel finally did the trick. We day-tripped to Killarney and Glendalough. We rode on jaunting cars drawn again by horses. I had two new dresses—both striped, one pink and one blue—which I loved and lived in. However, photos show that I did have other things to wear. Isabel tried her luck with the Irish sweepstake, which didn't work, and we wandered through Phoenix Park. This to me was abroad, something none of my friends had ever done. Wouldn't I have lots to tell when I got back? For some reason, I have no recollection of the journey home, which is strange as getting there is so vivid in my mind. Anyway, back we were. Nothing was mentioned about me leaving (well, not to me anyway) for the time being. The subject did come up later though.

Off to school for the autumn term, we had to write an essay or composition, as it was called then, about what we did in our holidays. I wrote pages on our trip to Ireland, omitting the part where I was sick. I also wrote about sitting on Netley Beach, watching the minesweepers in the Solent locating mines placed during the Second World War. I thought it fascinating. My friends and I had been moved several times by some official man in a uniform. Eventually, he decided we could stay at the risk of being blown up, which he said was preferable to listening to our protests about being moved, and as we were cheeky blighters, he couldn't be bothered with us any more. Well, obviously we survived, and after a lot of sticking out tongues and 'Nah na na nah nahs', we went home. My composition just said we sat on the beach watching minesweepers. I didn't feel the rest was appropriate. I wrote about learning to dance on ice after what seemed countless lessons. I also achieved several certificates. My composition/essay, which I thought would merit a good mark, got me nothing, not even a mention. Nothing unusual there then. The teacher probably couldn't read my scribble. I just went and did what I was good at—handstands against the wall.

Because of my skating skills, during the following winter, I was asked by my teacher at school if I could make a slide on the ice in the playground for everyone to try. (Can you imagine that happening now with health and safety?) I managed to make one about twelve feet long. The teachers and pupils enjoyed it very much, especially as it went downhill. I remember feeling so pleased with myself. It made up for the fact that academically speaking I was useless. My writing, which to me was scripted in the best possible way, merited a mark of three or four out of ten. Maths? Forget it. I was never going to be another Einstein, that's for sure. PE I loved. Anything that took me outside made me happy. However, the next day, a teacher, Mr Whiffin (nothing to do with the slide; he walked with a stick and could barely move), gave me the cane for talking in class. I called him old whiff bag under my breath and refused to cry. He didn't like girls very much and preferred to teach 'his boys', as he called them. I said boys were like toadstools; they stood around in clumps on the school playing field and were wet and thick. For that, I was sent to the head master. I was told to do a hundred lines of 'I must not be rude to a teacher'. Well, it had changed from 'I must not forget my PE kit' or 'I must learn to be more polite'. Isabel said she always knew where I was if I was late in getting home from school. I had become very skilled and adept at lines. It was all I did at school as far as I could remember—that and dodging the blackboard rubber as it came flying through the air.

My paternal grandmother passed away, and I was treated to seeing her body laid out in the sitting room, in her coffin. This apparently is what happened in those days. Heavens above, it was scary. She was covered in violets and primroses, which I was told were her favourite flowers. I have disliked them ever since. Not a good memory.

With more letters backwards and forwards between my aunt the NSPCC and George she decided enough was enough and couldn't cope any more. My uncle was threatening all the time towards her, saying why should they keep her brother's brat for nothing. My aunt tried to ask for more money from George. Nothing was forthcoming, so I came very close to being moved yet again. Slight reprieve, Isabel decided to stand up to her bully of a husband. It was her house from a previous marriage, and therefore, if she wanted me to stay, stay I would. We both cried a lot—her from despair, me from uncertainty. In hindsight, even more confusing to me was her pleading poverty. I would assume it was for George's benefit, because we went shopping for some material for a skating skirt for me, had a slight argument over which buttons to buy, and at the same time, she bought a mink coat. When we got back, after having paraded in front of the mirror for what seemed like hours, Isabel announced she didn't like it and took it across the road and gave it to her daughter. Because I was unaware of what was going on in the background, I didn't think anything of it. She did ask me what I thought and if it looked nice. I said yes, but how was I to know? It was just a furry coat, as far as I was concerned. I found out later it was mink. She already had one which smelt of moth balls, so why she bought another is anyone's guess.

Shortly after this episode, Isabel went on a cruise on the *Queen Mary*. Whilst she was away, she wrote to the NSPCC, saying she could no longer afford to keep me. She was not well and also had developed a cataract in one eye, which would entail an operation and a stay in the hospital. How things have changed. I have had two half-hour cataract operations. However, back then, it involved a much more complicated process. I stayed with her daughter (my cousin) who lived opposite whilst she was away. Grumpy fended for himself. Upon Isabel's return, my cousin, who already had two boys, said that I couldn't stay with her any longer as she couldn't cope with three children. Maybe at that time it was a trial run for me prior to living with them permanently. Who knows? I wasn't too popular there either.

Out of the blue, my sister(?) contacted me for the first time since my mother died to say that she was getting married and asked if I wanted to be a bridesmaid. I don't know I replied because I truly didn't know what I wanted to do. I hadn't seen her for years, and although I was quite small when she left home, I remembered she wasn't exactly pleasant to be around. This stemmed from the fact that she had to take me everywhere she went. Mum apparently said so. This didn't go down too well, especially if she was out with a boyfriend. I remember her dragging me across the kitchen floor by my hair on more than one occasion. In the years to come, things did change. More on that later. Anyway, I didn't get too excited, which was just as well because I heard nothing further from her for some time. The burgundy bridesmaid's dress (which was supposed to look lovely with my blonde hair) never materialized. She got married, and I wasn't there.

Meanwhile, unbeknown to me, the storm clouds were gathering. Several letters passed between George, Aunt Isabel, the Probation Service, and the NSPCC. I had been totally unaware of visits from a probation officer although records state there were many, with reports going between them all. I was described quite prolifically as varying from quiet and shy to rude and unresponsive. At the same time, I was in more trouble because a neighbour had asked me to do some shopping for her and gave me the money and said I was to take sixpence for myself. I returned with her goods and gave her the change minus the sixpence. However, she called my aunt and said I was a good-for-nothing little thief who had stolen her money. Unfortunately, my aunt chose to believe her, and no matter how much I protested my innocence, out came the wooden coat hanger again (why did no one spot these bruises?). In hindsight, I was a tomboy, always getting into scrapes, so maybe it was a given. By this time, after the death of my grandmother, my aunt had let our bedroom, so I was sharing with her and her husband. This was deemed unsuitable by the probation services and others involved, so this was the catalyst for the next stage of my life. It also coincided with having my long blonde hair (which I could sit on) cut off. The reason being, I was told, I was off to a children's home. I thought at the time, 'Doesn't anyone in a home have long hair then?' The notes state I was to be boarded out to Aunt Isabel. I had no idea what that meant except that if she felt better, I could go back to live with her. Sometimes, although as I have said before I was quite badly beaten, there were good times and also familiarity, which was somehow a comfort. Also, I would miss playing on the bomb sites and the freedom to run in the streets and play on makeshift carts made out of pram wheels. I suppose the endless lines I had to do at school and dreaming of *The Scarlet Pimpernel* could be done anywhere. However, I did find other things to get up to, as the next chapter tells you.

CHAPTER THREE

So here I am again on another strange doorstep, the door with shiny black paint, the clothes I had on and a carrier bag. My aunt had brought me to a Barnardo's home. We had gone through the office and registered, and I was allocated to Cambridge Cottage. Left behind were my ice skates, clothes, doll's pram, dolls, all my toys, and also a large box of ribbons of which I was very proud, having collected them when my hair was long. Now I had short hair, a squiffy fringe, and a hairgrip on one side. Add to that National Health glasses, and you have the picture. I said a fond farewell to Isabel and promised to write to her. I did, as I later found out, but didn't get any answers.

Greeted at the door by Matron and shown my bedroom, which I was to share, I left my meagre possessions on the bed and followed her into the dining room. Stuck on the wall were pictures of James Dean (no, I didn't know who he was either, although I do now), a film star and heart-throb of the time. He died young in a car crash, apparently, and was much loved by the resident nurse. She thought him dreamy. I was described as dreamy, but I think it meant uncooperative and unresponsive in my case. Matron appeared to be a quiet, unassuming lady who took her role seriously. She came from Ireland and didn't seem to have a lot of family to speak of. Looking back, she was so perfect for the job she had. As I had been to Ireland, she gave me a photo of herself taken in Glendalough, which I still have to this day. It is very small, and she is hardly visible, but I treasure it.

The first few days in Cambridge Cottage were a blur; however, as I had nothing with me, the first thing was clothing. There was a warehouse-type place that I was taken to and a very scary, badly scarred lady whom I couldn't take my eyes off. Kids, eh! She was obviously used to children looking at her because she didn't flinch. How sad for her, I thought. I wonder now if she was hurt during the war. I was given a new coat, dresses, skirts, blouses, underwear, etc. For some reason, probably due to my size 6 feet, they only had boy's shoes for me. These were the old-fashioned type with the toecaps, very uncomfortable but short-lived as I soon had others. However, the embarrassment at the time, having to wear these shoes to school, was hard.

I cannot stress enough how wonderful Matron was. She never raised her voice to anyone and was kind and loving. Many years later when I was interviewed to receive my records, I was asked how I was treated. I could honestly say, 'Extremely well.' I was told it wasn't the same for everyone as there were some very vicious house mothers. Fortunately, I didn't come across any myself. I ended up wondering, 'If they were cruel, how did they get away with it?' A sign of the times, I suppose.

I began to settle into the normal day-to-day routine. Matron's notes say that I was very shy, preferred the outdoors, and was amenable to discipline. She also said I had some intelligence. Where did that come from? So who were all the others talking about then? I was still monitored by the Social Services of the time, who noted that I was rude and sulked a lot and described me as monosyllabic, slow, and heavy. The last bit sounds like a carthorse. Maybe I responded differently to different people. Who knows? I cannot really remember.

School was painful for me. I was bullied verbally for coming from 'a home'. I was never picked for the netball team or for rounders. I spent a lot of time on the sidelines. Teachers were never interested in anything I had to say. Things I did in class, which I thought were worthy of a good mark, were never good enough. I felt I was just along for the ride. This wasn't helped by the fact that I was the only one not wearing a school uniform. When I asked Matron why I couldn't have one, she just said, 'Because you can't.' I later learnt I wasn't supposed to be staying. If my aunt couldn't have me back, I was going on to something more permanent, which would mean a change of school and uniform. Two other girls (twins), Joan and May, went to the same school. They were very popular, which made my isolation worse. Why did coming from a home not apply to them? Maybe as there were two of them, it was easier. Who knows? We always walked to school together, but I was never with them during playtime or lunchtime. The very interesting thing about this time is the fact that both Joan and May copied everything I did, from what I wore to my hair, and if I went swimming, they went too. They felt like my shadows out of school. Some years later I bought a brooch and earrings to match. These were in the shape of sheep—don't ask! I called the earrings Joan and May. Very immature!

I made up a poem about the teachers so I could remember their names, just for something to do really. I don't recall much of it, just these few words: 'It was a Hobday in the *Parish of Callaghan*. On the Vicar's doorstep stood a Gill of milk.' There was more, but this bit stuck in my head. Mrs Gill took my class for English, and I remember reading copious amounts of the *Mill on the Floss*, thinking at the time I was Maggie Tulliver.

The village home was built around a series of greens. The nursery, the reception (that was me), and the permanent. We had a wonderful hospital, our own church, and a swimming pool. We also had swings in front of Cambridge Cottage. Oh, and a very inviting-looking tree! I had a history of tree climbing and torn clothes, as I was constantly being reminded. Matron bought herself some lovely shoes. We had same-size feet, so she asked me to break them in for her. I did that, okay. I climbed the tree in them, got stuck at the top, and called for help, shoes badly scraped. Having climbed to what seemed a great height, I realized I couldn't get down. Matron came out and told me, or rather shouted up at me (the only time I heard her raise her voice), 'You got yourself up there, you get yourself down.' Then she promptly went back indoors. It was the first time since arriving that I had done something so stupid. It got darker and darker. I was getting colder and colder. I thought any minute she would get one of the house fathers to help me down. No such luck. In desperation, I started singing 'Ten Green Bottles' at the top of my voice, hoping to get on someone's nerves and keep myself warm. It didn't work, so I very gingerly picked my way down in the pitch-blackness with just the light from some cottage windows where they hadn't yet drawn the curtains, and found my way to the ground. I then sat on a swing which creaked with rusty chains, swinging my legs, shaking like a leaf, and feeling sorry for myself but, at the same time, having that old chestnut defiance. I was just about to launch into 'Ging Gang Goolie' (apologies to Lord Baden-Powell) when Matron came to get me. She said I could keep the shoes as I had ruined them. I sensed a smile on her face as I followed her indoors. I just had the feeling that she felt somehow pleased with herself for ignoring me, and if I was going to learn at all, this was the way to do it. It didn't work though!

According to our ages, we had pocket money which we could spend on sweets. We each had a jar on the kitchen windowsill with our names on. As I was the eldest, I was given eleven pence. I came back from my first outing with a bottle of clear nail polish. Matron said I was to put it on the windowsill where she could see it and asked if I knew that it wouldn't taste too good. 'Next time, fill your sweet jar' rang in my ears. I just said maybe one of the others would give me some of their sweets. She said she would make sure they didn't, followed by 'Shall we make a cake?' I was good at baking, if I may say so myself. Looking back, Matron was never going to let any of us beat her. It seemed she knew what we were up to before we did. I have to say I don't remember the other children doing too much wrong. It was just me for some reason. Was I trying to prove something? I don't know. I would love to go back and say sorry.

Most of the notes mention I was a tomboy and didn't look after my clothes. Some of my clothes were either sewn up or replaced. One particular afternoon I attached myself to the Romany gypsies camped opposite the home on a piece of waste ground. Twice I went off with them. For some reason, no one noticed I wasn't supposed to be part of the group. I was my usual scruffy self, so I fitted in quite well. I didn't get very far though. What on earth I thought I was doing, I have no idea. Both times, I was brought back by the police. I don't know how they found me, but they did.

We all had chores to do in the cottage. Mine was usually cake making and helping prepare meals. I was given the worst one for running away—shoe cleaning. This was done in all weathers outside under a lean-to attached to the back of the cottage. Matron said if I decided to run away again, she would move my bed down and I could live there as I liked the outdoors so much. I also lost the chance to bake in the kitchen, small punishment indeed for the mischief I caused, although I didn't think so at the time. I hated shoe cleaning! And I missed the warmth of the kitchen. Oh, and I was also on mousetrap duty. That was horrible. Well, to get my own back, I grabbed one poor, unfortunate dead creature by the tail and chased everyone around the kitchen with it. That got me off that particular duty. If I had known it was that easy to get out of emptying a trap every day, I would have done it sooner.

Sundays, oh, who could forget Sundays? Morning service, afternoon Sunday school, and evensong. God bothering, I called it, and I did say to Matron I was sure he could manage (God, that is) if I didn't go quite so often. I got to the stage where if I had to sing 'Jesus Wants Me for a Sunbeam' once more, I would scream. There were lots of things I wanted to be, and a sunbeam wasn't one of them. My reward, or should I say punishment, for this was to be taken to the church midweek, where a huge screen had been erected, to watch a film, *The Robe*. Anyone seen it? A religious epic. Well, you can understand why I tried to behave after that. I spent the whole two, or was it three, hours dreaming of what I would do when I got out of there. I was questioned by Matron and our nurse about the film and managed to bluff my way through with a few yeses, nos, and don't knows. They knew I hadn't paid much attention. I felt I was quite good at the blank look when I wanted to pretend I didn't know what anyone was talking about. I must have applied it then because Matron gave up.

Thursdays, we all looked forward to Thursdays. It was the day we had ice cream for tea (a post-war luxury), which had to be collected from the office by the main gate. We took turns to go and fetch it. One particular Thursday, it was howling a gale. It wasn't my turn to go; I had done it the previous week. Well, that's what I thought, but as I had been on the equivalent of the naughty step for a while, Matron said I was to go. No point protesting. I made a huge pantomime out of wrapping up in my coat, hat, and gloves, all to go probably 100 yards. I went off down the path with Matron asking why I made such a drama out of everything. Anyway, not long after that, I went down with a nasty dose of tonsillitis, and as we were in close contact with so many adults and children, I was put in isolation in the hospital. Apart from the fact that I felt really awful and had the most vile inky blue stuff to gargle with, I quite enjoyed my time there. Well, who wouldn't? No school, no bullying, no shoe cleaning, being waited on, lots of reading, and a nurse whom I had wrapped around my little finger. When I came back to Cambridge Cottage two weeks later, Matron said I was to go and see one of the house fathers (we had boys-only cottages). I asked, 'What for?' She wouldn't say, but she had obviously told him I was a drama queen.

It transpired he had written a play based on Aladdin, all in verse. I still remember some of it today. He asked if I wanted to be in it. I said yes as long as I could be the princess.

'Not much chance of that,' he said. 'You are too tall.'

So I said, 'No then.'

'Oh, so you don't want to be Aladdin?'

I said, 'I thought Aladdin was a boy!' (I didn't realize pantomimes swapped roles and gender.)

He did say, 'Given your antics up the tree the other night, I thought you were one.'

So I became Aladdin. I learnt the part very quickly and absolutely loved it. All of a sudden there I was performing on stage in front of an audience made up of children, teenagers, and adults. Did I feel important! We had a standing ovation, and I was told I looked like a young Grace Kelly. This was all contrary to being verbally bullied at school and not being included in anything and a feeling useless. I didn't know until much later this play was written especially with me in mind, which was why I got the starring role.

After this, a kind of arrogance grew in me, which I suppose, coupled with defiance, didn't actually endear me to many people. However, it helped me through the unhappy school days, which I struggled with. About this time, I was back in favour with Matron, heaven knows why. I was invited into her sitting room in the evenings to listen to *The Archers* along with a couple of others. I wanted to say, 'It really isn't for me, this everyday story of country folk. What use is that when you live in Barkingside?' but I didn't. She so obviously thought she was doing me a favour. There wasn't anything else to do, so I suppose I should be pleased. She also took me to see her friends who lived locally. Looking back, I wondered if she was lonely. We really did become firm friends. This stood me in good stead for my next misdemeanour, my worse time yet. I had got involved with some of the bigger boys who were going to the local Woolworths to shoplift. I don't know why I did it, but I joined in. I had a locker full of things I really didn't want—packs of playing cards, pens, pencils, rubbers, notepads, ink. It was so plain to see that these were not bought with my eleven pence a week. Matron somehow sorted all this out by taking me back to the store with the things I had taken and making me apologize, which I did, and at the time, I think I got off lightly! Shoe cleaning again, no cinema, and definitely no youth club, where I had got involved with the boys in the first place. I didn't end up living in the lean-to though. I am so ashamed of this now, but I mention it as part of my life growing up.

These boys were extremely cruel to me whenever I saw them, usually at the swimming pool. They would go into my changing cubicle and take my clothes, sometimes throwing them in the pool and making fun of my newly acquired bra. I was left shivering and had to walk home in my swimming costume whilst they stood around laughing. They thought I had told on them. I hadn't, because their house father was as suspicious as Matron when they paraded their spoils in front of everyone.

We were all assembled for a good talking-to by the local policeman. I can't speak for them, but it scared me witless. Different policeman though from the one that brought me back from my gypsy foray. Like I have said before, all the others I lived with seemed so good. They were younger. I suppose that helped. Never mind, Matron would probably have been bored to tears if I hadn't been around. On the other hand, her life would have been a whole lot easier. How on earth I didn't end up with a criminal record, I will never know.

So my life in Barnardo's continued, and as I grew up, I suppose I might have been more sensible. Our resident nurse and her boyfriend (who looked nothing like James Dean or dreamy) would take us for picnics. We nicknamed him Muscles because she would carry everything and he trailed behind, looking as if he would rather be somewhere else. He was quite good at football though, or should I say kicking about, because that is how we passed our time in the park. We were also taken to the cinema on the odd occasion.

Once a year the London black-cab drivers would give a day of their time and take us to the seaside. We were so excited to see them lined up along the drive and around the green. The lead taxi was always decorated in streamers and balloons. I remember being in this one once. Our photo appeared on the front page of the *Daily Sketch* (I have searched the archived papers but have been unable to find it). We were waving out of the window at everybody, having the time of our lives. These are fond memories for me. We went to Clacton. I do think I was slightly embarrassed though because there was a large group of us. Someone erected a flag on the beach, which we all had to cluster around for our instructions and where we had to come back to. This was one of the occasions I felt different from everyone else. It was a sensible way to make sure no one got lost, but I wasn't thinking of that at the time. I was half listening but had my eye on the roller coaster called Steel Stella. I managed to persuade Matron to come on it with me. She looked quite green when she got off. Well, it was the least she could do when I had been subjected to *The Archers* every evening. That is a twelve-year-old's thinking!

I had not heard from any of my family(?). I use this term loosely because I didn't know if they were or not, and I still don't to this day. I just felt sure about my maternal grandmother, and that was it. However, I was told I could go to stay with Isabel for a couple of days and travel by train, under the charge of the guard. Yes, that's what happened back then. He would look after me during the journey and make sure I got off at the right station. So I was off to Southampton, feeling very grown-up. During the journey, I was talking to a lady who said her name was Mary. I have a hazy memory of the conversation; however, it transpired that I told her I lived in Barnardo's. She wanted to befriend me and have me stay with her and her husband. She must have been serious because I did stay with them sometimes. They proved to be my saviour of sorts. I will explain later on. However, back to my trip to Isabel's. Not too much to report on this visit. We went to the shops. Isabel bought herself a blouse. I desperately wanted a picture skirt. They were very fashionable at the time and depicted various scenes in pastel shades and were very pretty. Isabel said it wasn't suitable and bought me a paisley-patterned pinafore dress instead. I thought it was awful. However, a few years later, when I had a job as a department store model, guess what my first outfit was? A picture skirt, back in fashion for the second time around. The rest of this visit is very vague, not too much in my notes either.

I went back to Barnardo's, clutching my new dress, but I didn't remember wearing it, although I do have one photo of myself in it. Not long after this, there was talk of Australia. A lot of children were sent away if they didn't have a family. I believe thousands went. I knew I was on the list. I expect Matron made sure of that. I was sent for a medical—survival of the fittest, methinks! However, I had crooked toes, and it was decided I wasn't fit to go. Besides, as I said previously, I had a family of sorts. I remember the excitement of those that were going, having been promised Christmas on the ship. I think I had a lucky escape, having read the later reports of what happened to these children. It didn't sound too pleasant. I wasn't very popular in a small community, so how on earth I would get by on a huge liner is anyone's guess! I would probably end up in the hold, sharing leg irons with a convict.

Back to Mary, she and her husband, John, had contacted Barnardo's with a view to having me stay some weekends. They lived in Highgate in London, in what to me seemed a huge apartment. We had so much fun. They took me to all the sights. The Tower of London (no, they didn't leave me there) was my favourite. However, Mary did express concern over my lack of communication with John. He felt upset that I ignored him a lot of the time. I suppose my history with the men in my life hadn't been very positive. I hadn't known at the time that John had a very high-powered job in the government, which, as I have said before did help me later on.

They knew I was keen on sports and bought me my very own netball and a tin of dubbin (I remember that it smelt awful) to wax and care for the leather ball. I made the huge mistake of taking it to school. I naively thought I might just be included in a game if I had my own ball. I had hung it over my chair in its net. This was stolen in class, and although I saw others playing with it, I never got it back. Matron did get a little cross and said I shouldn't have taken it. How could I explain to her that I just wanted to be included in things and, at least, have some friends? It was not until later I discovered that this isn't how it works. People/children either like you or they don't. Netballs will not buy anyone.

I heard talk of foster parents. I knew something about what this entailed. I had two runs at it, to begin with; neither worked out. I remember one family trying to get me to go to bed. As I wouldn't budge, they recorded a message on a tape recorder, saying, 'Jeanette, it is time for bed.' They kept playing this until I gave in and went upstairs. This was all very well, but I didn't get it. 'Why would I want to be with a strange family?' I said so at the time. No surprise, I didn't go to either again.

However, the time came for me to leave my safe haven at Barnardo's. I said a tearful farewell to Matron and promised to visit. I never did. It was just before my fourteenth birthday. I had no idea why I needed to go as there were older teenagers still there. However, I assumed as I was placed in the reception that it was just a temporary home for me, and I had to move on somehow. Also, I hadn't realized until much later that my movements were still monitored by Barnardo's. Even though I had left, I was still in their care until I reached eighteen years old. This came as a great surprise to me when I received and read my records.

CHAPTER FOUR

I was to be placed with an older couple who had an adopted son and ran a pub. I never had seen or met these people before. The vetting system could not have been as stringent as it is today. To me, it was the most unsuitable place to put a teenager in, though it all seemed okay to start with. Schooling again wasn't too good. By this time, I had grown very tall, about five feet ten inches. I was called all sorts of names from lamp post to matchstick and was generally ignored. Also academically, I hadn't improved much. Now I had needlework classes to contend with. My teacher said I wasn't very good at sewing, but I did my best. Then we had country dancing classes too. Oh, 'Help' is all I can say on that one. I either set off before the music or turned the wrong way and bumped into the girl next to me. This was not a good time, adjusting again to a new regime. I did join the church choir and made friends with Rene, whom I met in church and who also sang in the choir. We were very close. We had such a good time and went everywhere together. She made my life bearable; however, I repaid her kindness by stealing her boyfriend! For some reason, she was fine about it. Perhaps I did her a favour. Who knows? And we remained good friends for the duration of my stay. Barnardo's was insisting I was to be christened. I didn't know I wasn't; however, this was arranged at the local church. It seemed very strange hanging my head over the font at fourteen years of age; however, I liked the reverend, whom I got to know from my time in the choir. He was a very kind and caring elderly gentleman with a lovely name, Reverend Badger. And I don't think he wanted me for a sunbeam!

The pub was in a small village. I mentioned new regime; there wasn't one really. I was left mainly to my own devices, ignored most of the time. Life in the pub meant my foster parents had very little time for me. I lived on pork pies and crisps with the occasional cooked meal. We had a spaniel called Major, whom I walked every day after school and weekends, but apart from joining the guides and my friends, I was quite lonely. My foster mother said I was sullen and joyless—a couple of labels to go with the rest. It was difficult to be anything with nothing to respond to. They never took me anywhere, and we didn't do anything as a family. I didn't really feel comfortable with them, and I felt abandoned to fate. My foster brother had a really nice girlfriend, whom I befriended and spent some time with, but that was it. Then the unthinkable happened. Out of the blue, my foster father began doing really odd things. He would leave magazines laying about with scantily dressed women on the covers. He began to draw on these covers inappropriate pictures and write my name on them, leaving them around for me to see. He would also leave explicit notes in my room, which I tried to avoid reading. The worst things that happened were at night. He would lie in his bed next to my room and call me to go to him. I would pretend not to hear, and I remember one night pretending to be asleep. I was desperate to move because the dog, which insisted on sleeping on my bed, had lain across my head. He kept saying, 'I know you can hear me, come to bed with me.' I had never been so scared in all my life. I plucked up the courage to speak to my foster mother, who told me I was imagining it all and not to be so stupid. She made a point of going to play bridge some evenings with a neighbour. I think now she knew what was going on. How could she not have seen the magazines? Also, she must have known he came to bed before her, and if she was in, she must have heard him calling me. At the time, I was so scared and couldn't say any more to anyone. I didn't know how to deal with it. I remember I froze with fear when I heard the stairs and floorboards creak as he came upstairs. He never came into my room whilst I was there, but the terrifying sound of his voice whispering to me made me feel sick. I thought it was my fault or that, as my foster mother said, I imagined it all. If she was so sure I was making up stories, why didn't she speak to the authorities? As far as I know, she didn't mention it to anyone, which, looking back, didn't make any sense to me.

However, the last straw was when she said she was going away with the Bridge Club. I confided in a friendly dinner lady at school who had picked up on the fact that things were not right. She said I looked ill and very sad. Although at the time I didn't realize it, there had been some dispute over money again. I was still wearing the badly scraped shoes Matron had given me. By this time, they were very much down at the heels, but I was given some really nice clothes by some neighbours, including a riding mac, which I loved and lived in. My foster parents had not spent on me the allowance they had been given by Barnardo's. It was reported that I was badly dressed and uncared for. For the first time, someone had noticed things were not right. Rene had asked me on several occasions why I had badly worn shoes and no clothes to speak of. I didn't know at the time that the foster parents (I use this term loosely) did not spend anything on me at all. It is an understatement to say that this was not a good time for me. Whilst being happy with my boyfriend and his lovely family, enjoying the freedom I had, and singing in the church choir on a Sunday, it was also a time of extreme fear. These people were not the kind and caring type. I don't, to this day, know why I was even placed with them. What possible use was I except for the abuse from my foster father and neglect by my foster mother? Was that it? Was that why

I was there? I think so now, looking back. I don't know if anything was done about this couple and the way they treated me. I would like to think they were punished in some way. I never saw them again.

I was so relieved when I was moved to the friendly dinner lady whose daughter had befriended me at school.

I cannot believe how lucky I was. I had lovely clean clothes. My hair (which by now had grown) was clean and tidy. Altogether, life seemed so much better. I suppose, in comparison, I was quite spoilt, although I didn't realize how much at the time. A leopard doesn't change its spots though, and I think I was still quite a difficult child. Overall though, my schoolwork improved, and I made more friends. I joined the local youth club. Oh and hey, back to church, only once on a Sunday though. I joined this choir and was chosen to sing a solo, Psalm 23, which seemed to be appreciated by the congregation. Well, none walked out anyway, and I got a weak smile from the organist.

I didn't see much of my new foster father. It was a bit strange really. He bred these huge lop-eared rabbits, but he didn't like anyone going too near them. They were prize winners, he said. I didn't see it myself. They were just big fat things with big floppy ears. He featured very little in my life. I don't have much memory of him, just the occasional conversation whilst he checked his beloved rabbits.

I was told I had to stay on at school. I said no, that I needed to get a job. 'No, Jeanette, you stay at school. At least get some education behind you.' Well, it hadn't worked so far, so there wasn't much chance of me ever achieving notoriety on that score. Well, I knew best and ended up at the local International Stores filling shelves. Good move? I don't think so. What I hadn't realized was, I was now going to have to pay for myself and give my foster parents board and lodging monies. The figures quoted in a letter addressed to me from Barnardo's are as follows. And I quote:

Dear Jeanette,

I am writing to let you know that as you are not quite earning enough to cover your expenses we are going to help you. Ms Smith told us you have commenced work and your earnings are £2 18s a week. Your expenses are Board £1 10s, fares 6s 0d, tea 1s 2d National Insurance 4s 8d in addition we feel you should have a £1 for yourself that is 10/—pocket money and 10/—to put away for clothes this means you require £3 1s 10d per week, which is 3s 10d more than you earn. Will you therefore give your Foster mother 26/—and we will send the remaining 4s 0d. I hope you enjoy your work.

Forgive me if the figures do not add up. I have just copied the letter as it reads. Even though I realize now this is kindness itself, I had the feeling I had blotted my copybook. I couldn't give up the fighting spirit even when it wasn't needed. I still felt I was the one who knew best, only I didn't really. I hated the job and hoped I would get the sack. Much to my surprise, my 'brother' appeared. I don't know how he knew where I was. He asked if I would like to go for the weekend with him and his wife and family, whom I had never met and didn't know existed. Anyway, I said yes and went home to tell my foster mother. She turned to me exasperated and said that at fourteen years old I could not decide where and what I did without asking her first. Did I not realize she was responsible for me and I needed permission to go anywhere? Well, I didn't actually! I was reported to my social worker and got the same from her. Oh, whoops. Well, if you are not told, you wouldn't know, would you? Headstrong, I think they call it. However, George (yes, that was his name too) collected me from work the next day, and I spent a nice weekend with him and his family. Who were all these people? I seemed to be constantly on the move from one person to another. I felt no closeness to George or his family. We hadn't grown up together, so to me, he was a stranger. I didn't say this to him, but I did wonder why he was back in my life again.

Back home again, I didn't do too well at work. Filling shelves was boring. I and another girl would open the cereal packets to take the free gifts out—some sort of plastic rubbish we didn't want. Then I dropped a whole tray of jam—a sticky mess all over the stockroom floor. I was told to go home and not come back. That was the end of my job. I didn't know whether to be happy or sad. I did lose face, however, and felt embarrassed. I had already been sacked from a school-holiday job picking tomatoes. Greenhouses are not the best place to work in the height of summer. Then I decided I wanted to work with children. The powers that be said I needed to go back to school. I said I didn't. So the search for a suitable 'mother's help' work started.

I had the feeling, given the comments, that this was a time when some of those who cared for me were giving up. My records state that I should now be left to do what I wanted— every teenager's dream—but I hadn't realized at the time what these caring individuals had done for me. We had gone to West Wittering for a holiday and stayed on a farm in a caravan. My new foster mother had made me some dresses, which were lovely, and I attracted the attention of a local lad who would wait at the farm gate to see me. My foster mother allowed him to come out with us on day trips and actively encouraged us to spend time together. When we were due home, she said that he could come and stay with us. For some reason which I couldn't explain, I didn't know how to deal with this. I was far too young for this kind of commitment. My foster mother, being kindness itself, said not to let on that I was fostered but to say that I was her adopted daughter;

however, the lad got a glimpse of my glasses case, in which I had written my name, and asked why I was Jackson-Smith and the rest of the family were Stevens. Cover blown, although he didn't seem that bothered when I told the truth. A week before he was due to visit, I wrote to ask him not to come, and I never heard from him again. I still remember him writing 'I love you' in the sand and the marcasite earrings he bought me. It just all seemed too much at the time. Why couldn't I see what I had? I don't know. I just had this urge to move on. What to? I had no idea. I just found it difficult to stay in one place too long. I suppose, given my history, this was not surprising.

CHAPTER FIVE

Eventually, after much searching, a live-in position as a mother's help came up. The family visited us. I met the two little boys I was to care for. We got on famously, and I was employed to look after them—one just over a year, and the other, four. I was fifteen years old. However, I did feel quite grown-up. My notes read that my new employer had been told what was felt by the authorities to be relevant; also stated is the fact that I was completely aware of what I was taking on.

They lived in a hamlet in Surrey; however, when my social worker took me to their home, my heart sank. They lived in the middle of nowhere, surrounded by a wood. The drive to their cottage was endless, and I knew I would have a problem getting anywhere. Hansel and Gretel came to mind when I saw their cottage. The worst bit (and I still hate them to this day) was an empty swimming pool. I feel there is something creepy about an empty hole which is supposed to be filled with water. A huge catamaran filled the garage along with a van, which I felt would look better on a scrap heap. An odd picture, a shiny boat and a rusty vehicle. I was to work six days a week and choose which day I would like off.

My room is described as comfortable with a single bed, dressing table, and armchair. 'Unable to swing a cat' sprang to mind. I couldn't spend too much time in it without getting cabin fever.

Because I had no means of getting anywhere on my day off and mooned around the house, as my employers called it, I was made to work. So seven days it was, until I acquired a cycle. I had dreamt for years about owning a bicycle, but the boneshaker I was given didn't really fit the dream. Even then, there was nowhere to go except to the forester's house further into the woods. I only came across that by accident, following the sound of a saw. I made friends with a girl who lived there. She felt as isolated as I did. I looked after the boys, whom I loved. I took them for long walks in the woods. We had a lot of fun together. Although the family employed a cleaner, I was to do the odd bit of housework and the ironing. Mr Jones worked in the city as a stockbroker. I had to iron his shirts and hang them up for his inspection before putting them away, coupled with walking their dog, sweeping up copious leaves, and wheelbarrowing huge loads of logs. I didn't have a lot of time to myself. However, I earned a wage, and Mrs Jones would take me to Haslemere to do some shopping occasionally. There is some indication in my notes that they were anticipating leaving me at weekends with the boys whilst they went sailing. It seems, looking back, they wanted cheap labour and a babysitter. I would not have been happy in that isolated place on my own with the children.

I found out later, they had been through a few live-in nannies.

They went on a skiing holiday at Christmas, leaving me and the children with Mrs Jones's mother, who lived in Weybridge.

A misunderstanding led to another problem for me. Mrs Jones's mother said she would pay for me to have my hair done as a Christmas present. 'Oh goody, can I have a perm, please?' This was to be my downfall because when I came back, both boys burst into tears when they saw me and cowered in a corner. 'Oh, dear,' Grandma said, 'they don't recognize you. They will soon get used to your new hairstyle.' Only it wasn't translated in this manner to Mr and Mrs Jones. She told them the children were frightened of me and shouldn't be in my care.

I disliked her house. It was an ill-kept old Edwardian place which was cold and uninviting. Brown lino everywhere with a row of bells still in place, used in past years to call servants. My room was huge, cold, and what I would term unfriendly. I couldn't wait to get up and out in the morning. The boys got used to me again, although we had an uneasy truce. When we got back to the cottage, Mr and Mrs Jones held a cocktail party (this was a new one for me; what the dickens was a cocktail party?) for some very influential clients, and I was to be the door girl, coat taker, and drinks hander-outer. I was well briefed for over an hour on how to behave. Well, name-dropper extraordinaire me, the clients were Christina and Aristotle Onassis. What a shame I wasn't old enough, intelligent enough, or clued up enough to know who these people were. It was all to do with Mr Jones's work in the city with British Steel and the shipbuilding industry, apparently.

After this, I could tell I wasn't wanted any more. Mrs Jones obviously needed me to know this because she left notes on her desk for me to see. These mostly said that she would be glad when I left, and when the time finally came for me to leave, she had written, 'Jeanette goes soon. Hurrah.' However, it wasn't solely that. John and Mary had somehow got wind of the fact that I was being what they called exploited, and at fifteen I should not have that kind of responsibilities on my shoulders. John had contacted the home office and asked them to intervene because of the way I was treated. They had visited me and apparently were quite perturbed by what they found. At this time, Mary was pregnant (although I didn't know), and they were moving out of London and were not in a position to have me with them. The next best thing was to try to sort something out for me. This was another period of uncertainty. I hadn't realized it at the time, but according to my notes, I was looking for other work and indeed had written to several people regarding what we called live-in jobs. I had tried so hard to make this work for me as I adored the boys. I would think, out of everyone in this story, they are the two that would still be alive. I often wonder where they are and what happened to them. I have tried tracing them, but no luck. I would love to see and speak to them again.

I do find the authorities' version of events here at odds with what I remember. I wasn't able to get out much. Mrs Jones said she came for walks with us in the woods and took me backwards and forwards to the youth club. Also, she said I wouldn't go anywhere without her. Well, apart from the fact that I couldn't go far anyway unless she took me in the car, what was I supposed to do?

I don't remember much about leaving, which is probably just as well because I know I would be very sad. I wouldn't miss the isolation or the loneliness, but I would miss the two little boys.

My sister was somehow located and asked to take responsibility for me. She agreed but only till another home-help job was found. It had been agreed, although I didn't know it, and a room had been booked for me in a girl's hostel in Oxford at a cost of 3s. 10d. a week. However, the Barnardo's aftercare team did not agree with this idea because they thought I might get used to it, and they were not prepared to pay out this much on a long-term basis. It was also stated that an interview had been set up for me as a home help (live-in) somewhere in North Oxford to care for two little girls aged seven and five and some housework. Well, I wasn't doing anyone's housework, which I made quite clear, so that idea went down the pan.

CHAPTER SIX

I arrived in Oxford just short of my sixteenth birthday and was met at the bus station by my sister and her husband. My notes state that she wanted to have me live with or near them and would take care of me. This I felt wasn't strictly true, and again things went from bad to worse.

I knew from the start that this was not going to be an easy time. I cannot remember if I knew that my sister (I use the term loosely) and her husband lived in a caravan. We were not small people, so this proved extremely difficult. They bickered and argued the whole time, and I lived on a knife-edge, frightened to say anything. My brother-in-law was a quiet, genial man, but it was just an awful time. Coupled with this, my sister found me a job working with her. I didn't really know, looking back, what it was all about. She worked the switchboard, and I did general office work, mainly in accounts. It was okay from what I remember, but I wasn't happy. Living and working together did not bode well. We hardly knew each other and had not spoken for years. To this day, I wonder about this relationship. I was not her favourite person, but sometimes, there was a glimpse of what it could be like. We would go swimming in the local river at lunchtimes, laugh together, and make ourselves presentable again for going back to work. Then a silence would descend, and she wouldn't speak again unless she was shouting about something.

It was eventually decided that our living arrangements were unsuitable. My sister and brother-in-law had bought a house which needed a lot of work. This was being done whilst they remained in the caravan. I was relocated again! To a neighbour a mile or so up the road. A small bungalow, no running hot water or bathroom, just a toilet. I think I lived in more places in my short life than most people do in a lifetime.

So here I was, ensconced with another couple who to me seemed quite old, although they were probably not because both were working. My aftercare team was paying these people £2. 10s. a week to care for me. I hated not having a bath. I had a jug and a washbasin in my room and doused myself and the floor down every morning in water heated from a kettle. I had a deodorant which older readers might remember, called Body Mist in a mauve plastic squirty bottle. What didn't go in my armpit went up my nose. This was meant to be a short-term arrangement. This is where my notes go awry because they say I was staying with these people until a suitable job was found. I already had work in Oxford with my sister, which I mentioned before. Maybe it means they were looking for live-in jobs on my behalf. It was not made very clear.

At this time, I had sad news. Isabel had passed away and her husband a month earlier. Sorry to say, I wasn't too sad about him, but I was really upset about my aunt. At about this time, I also heard that my maternal grandmother had passed away too. I had loved and lost the people I cared most about at a young age.

I decided to enrol in a secretarial college in Oxford as I was earning £4 a week and some money from my coffee shop modelling in a local department store. (Remember the picture skirt? Come on, keep up!) However, I hadn't taken into account, as I was working and earning, that I would need to pay my board and keep. Why was I, and still am, so useless with money? Anyway, the upshot is, the aftercare stepped in again and paid half my college fees, which worked out okay because I only did half the work! Typing was good, but I spent shorthand evenings in the local Wimpy bar.

My report from work was pleasing and music to my social worker's ears. My sister had moved on to another job at the local hospital, so I was office worker and temporary switchboard operator. I honed my telephone voice to perfection.

Well, it was 20 April 1960, and the ball was still bouncing, this time between Oxford City Council Children's Department, my sister, the people I lodged with, and my social worker. Oh, and also my employers, who surprisingly were still very pleased with me.

Sad to say, this period of stability didn't last too long. I met a boy whom I will call Peter. He had spent some time with the people I was staying with, and they regarded him as their son. We were just friends; we would watch television, play records, and go out on his motorbike.

On 24 April 1960, it is noted that my sister would be moving into her house soon, and I had been invited to live with them. However, this didn't happen immediately.

Some friction had developed between my sister and the people I lived with about my friendship with Peter. Apparently, we were all going on a holiday together, and my sister wasn't too happy about it. However, it seems I had permission to go. I don't remember too much about it, but I presume it went okay. The Girls Aftercare Department stated that although they sided with my sister, they couldn't really ask that the arrangements be cancelled at the eleventh hour; however, they wanted to cover their tracks in case anything happened whilst we were away. They had also been asked to consult with my sister about her fears regarding my friendship with Peter and asked if there was something she knew that she wasn't telling.

On 14 November, I was still in my lodgings, and it seemed my sister had decided it might be better if I didn't live with them after all. She was very anxious about my friendship with Peter, and it was causing some angst in everyone.

In everyone's general opinion, Peter had fallen for me as I was a very attractive girl; however, I had been advised to keep the friendship light, and I was pretty well able to take care of myself.

More problems arose between my sister and the couple I lodged with, the consequence of which was another move (if they put me in an Arab dress and stuck me on a camel, I couldn't be more of a nomad), so I was now living with my sister's neighbour.

I have thought long and hard as to how to progress with the rest of this story. It is a sensitive and even more difficult time in my life.

I had been ill for some time—sickness, fainting fits, and extreme stress. The doctor had diagnosed gastroenteritis, but I felt dreadful. I carried on with my typing classes and work and somehow survived.

I will not go into too much detail; however, five months down the line, when I could stand it no longer, the doctor told me I was pregnant. My feelings at this stage were a mixture of relief to have the cause of my illness identified and fright along with sadness. What on earth was I going to do? I was in enough trouble already, so this would not be good.

As I have said, not too much detail, but this wasn't my fault. I will not name the protagonist or exactly what happened, but I am sure readers will draw their own conclusions. Besides which I made sure he disappeared from my life.

I was due to live with my sister and her husband. I eventually moved in with them for a short time.

I was taken to the hospital for antenatal checks and to book a bed. However, I was told by Girls Aftercare that I was to move away from the area as my sister didn't want me. I think she made that perfectly clear during the short time I stayed with her. She worked at another local hospital in the records department and didn't want anyone knowing I was her pregnant sister. I was mostly ignored, never taken out with them, and spent long weekends on my own, sometimes whilst they visited friends. I don't blame them for this as it must have been a very difficult time for them too.

There was some talk of my sister adopting my child; however, it was decided it wasn't a good idea. Besides which, I had said I would not part with my baby. Also, on one occasion, she had hit me very hard. I contacted my care worker, who also had a call from my sister saying how sorry she was. My notes say the contrary, but also, the powers that be were already putting the adoption process in place. I wasn't aware of this until I read my notes.

It is the old carrot-and-stick scenario again. They were kind and caring, doing everything to help me, but plotting my future with no discussion with me as to how I felt. In fact, part of my notes says, 'Who knows how Jeanette truly feels?' They just had to ask!

CHAPTER SEVEN

I was eventually sent to a mother-and-baby home. Again, I felt I was the odd one out. I couldn't relate to anyone. We were all of an age and in the same boat, but for some reason, I was accused of being stand-offish and told that just because I worked in an office, it didn't make me any better than anyone else. Well, I already knew that. Besides which, most girls had letters, presents, and visits from family. I had nothing and no one, so believe me, I was under no illusions about myself. I was also very withdrawn and worried about what was happening and where we were going to end up, so maybe I did appear to be remote. That just reflected how I felt.

The home was a spartan and bleak place. A huge monstrosity as I remember it. Cold and dark. However, we were well cared for, and each was allocated chores. We had dormitory bedrooms. I don't have any recollection of whom I shared with. A lot of my time here is a blank. My health improved, but my demeanour didn't. I had my maternity benefit, which I collected from the post office once a week, out of which I had to pay the home. I didn't have a lot left, but I didn't really need anything.

We were all examined every Thursday by the local doctor. Nothing unusual there, but it did feel like a conveyor belt. 'Come on, your turn next.'

There is no humour to be found in being pregnant, unmarried, and in a stark maternity home which was completely hapless and very uncomfortable physically and emotionally. There was no one to talk to. I just went along with the rules and regulations of the place. Yes, I did comply for once in my life.

One morning some weeks later, I awoke at 5 a.m. with a mild ache in the pit of my stomach. I felt very uncomfortable and got up to walk around. The floorboards creaked, and I worried I would wake the rest of the occupants. The surrounding space felt eerie and unfriendly. Apart from the noisy floorboards, the place was silent. I got back to bed, shivering and shaking, thinking, 'Is this it? Is my baby coming?' The pains grew stronger but not unbearable, so I laid there till it was time to go for breakfast.

I went to find Matron. By this time, it was around 9.30 a.m., and we were due for a check-up by the doctor at roughly 10 a.m. I was told to go first. Matron announced me by saying, 'This one thinks she is in labour.' I recall thinking, 'My name is Jeanette, and I know I am in labour.' However, I kept my mouth shut, and the doctor confirmed I was well on the way to giving birth.

I was taken to what was called the delivery room, which was just an ordinary bedroom with a single bed in the corner and a cot under the window. Assisted by pethidine (a painkiller) and Matron, I gave birth to my little girl. Matron placed her in the cot and told me to rest. I sat up in bed, talking to my baby and telling her we would be okay, that I would love her and look after her for the rest of my life, and if she could please stop sucking her fingers as she would make them sore.

We were moved to what was called the hospital wing, where we would spend the next two weeks. The rules were such that babies were only brought to their mothers for feeding and changing; the rest was overseen by a nurse.

I hadn't ever experienced such an overwhelming love as I did for my child. It was me and her against the world. I felt I had at last got something to live and care for that was mine. I set about thinking how we would manage. Adoption was never mentioned, and I couldn't part with her anyway. When my social worker visited, she saw us both and remarked on what a beautiful baby my daughter was. I felt proud to bursting.

After two weeks I was moved back to the dormitory bedroom and tried to make some arrangements to take my daughter home. I applied for live-in work, but nobody wanted an unmarried mother and her baby. My sister had already made it clear she didn't want me back, and who could blame her?

One day after morning feed, we were in the nursery. I was singing nursery rhymes to my little girl as she went to sleep in my arms. The nurse came in and said that it was time for her weekly weighing. I was reluctant to hand her over as I didn't want to wake her. I did though, and as she was carried out of the room, her little face peered over the nurse's shoulder. I waved and said, 'I will see you soon.' I waited for her to come back. The nursery fell silent. The other mothers had gone, and I just sat there waiting and waiting.

I never saw my daughter again. I felt as if my heart had been ripped out. I wandered the corridors, searching and calling to no avail. I was told that as I had no home to go to and no means of supporting her, she had gone for adoption. This was not the Dark Ages, just England in the early sixties.

I thought I was going to die. I couldn't breathe, had panic attacks, and really believed my life was over. Then I was told that I was leaving to live with my sister. So now that my baby had gone, I was invited back to them. Small consolation.

I sobbed and sobbed until there were no more tears. I didn't really care where I went. How was going back to my sister going to help? I didn't want to see the next day, let alone look into any future someone might have planned for me.

Did the Social Services, Aftercare Department, or anyone else for that matter really know what they had done? I really don't think they did. I was a case study, a commodity, costing money and time.

There were the odd glimpses of compassion in my records; however, I was just one of a large number of boys and girls they were caring for.

CHAPTER EIGHT

My sister was sent £2 for my board and keep and best wishes for taking me back. Also, I had an interview arranged for me as a typist/clerk in an office. Well, I got the job, and whilst I felt dreadful and bereft, I carried on. I did my job to the best of my ability. I didn't know what bought ledger was, let alone how to do it, but somehow I managed and got by. I was earning £4. 5s. a week and paying £1. 5s. for board and keep. Apparently, this was okay with my sister but not considered enough by Girls Aftercare. They were sending a subsidy to my sister of 10/—a week so I could keep the rest of my money to buy some clothes. I had become very thin and had nothing much to wear. After three months, I was to pay 35/-.

According to my notes, things were going along quite nicely, but I did not seem to be able to provide my own entertainment (didn't anyone realize how I felt?). The last thing I wanted to do was go out anywhere. Every child I saw was mine. Every baby in a pram was mine. I could not get her beautiful face out of my mind.

Also stated was that my sister had to take me to bingo. Had to? I don't think so. I fully remember her asking me to go with her as she had no one to go with. It is also stated that she took me to the local youth club. Actually, I took myself. I had always wanted to be a dancer, so I joined a dancing class too. This was all in the forefront of what was really going on in my mind. Where was my baby?

There was talk of another move. Things were not working out with my sister and her husband. Barnardo's Aftercare was trying to arrange for me to move into a bedsit with another girl who was having problems with her family. Because we were both under eighteen years old, this was considered inadvisable and quickly discounted.

I was informed I would have to find another job which paid more money. I thought I earned enough, and besides which, it was the average salary at the time. It was also suggested I take shorthand lessons. It had obviously been forgotten. I was supposed to be doing them at college before when I chose to go to the local Wimpy bar.

Several options for me had been explored. Nothing affordable in the bedsit department had come up. However, I had been very helpful over Christmas apparently, so at least I had pleased my sister but not anyone else. As my notes say, 'No one knows how long this will last.'

A letter from Barnardo's states that I didn't get the job in the bank I went for. How on earth could I think I could work in a bank when as far as I was concerned, two and two made five? I had no idea. I don't recall going for an interview, but I must have done. I was now due to move to a room found for me by my care worker.

The cost was £2. 10s. a week. Breaking down my expenses, it was agreed that Barnardo's Aftercare would subsidize my wages.

A stern letter to my social worker from Barnardo's Aftercare says that she hadn't made it clear to me that I need to find a better-paying job as they no longer wished to subsidize my wages any more. The one thing I learnt from my notes, which makes me very angry, is that my landlady was taking full rent from me as well as the subsidy from Barnardo's. I was only supposed to pay £1. 15s. Instead, I paid the full £2. 10s. whilst she received the extra money too. I didn't know about the money she was getting and never thought to mention to my social worker how much I was paying. I just remember being asked to babysit in exchange for my rent occasionally. No wonder they were anxious that I find a better-paying work. I eventually moved to a larger room to share. Also, I managed to find a telephonists job with more pay at a local car factory.

At this stage, my records state I was very thin. This was not surprising as I couldn't afford to eat. I lived solely on the roll and cake we were given at work every day. Also, apparently, I wore very tight and short clothes. I wore the things I was given by friends. I didn't have the money to buy new.

Well, no more carrot and stick, no bouncing ball. I had put my grieving for my daughter in a box in my head. I could open this when I wanted to, and now I felt some kind of comfort and thought of the phrase 'Don't cry because I am no longer with you, smile because I am'.

I had several opportunities for a boyfriend, but I really didn't want anyone in my life. They would share my memories, and I didn't want that. I wanted to keep my memories safe for me alone. Of course, things did change.

A couple of years later and earning more money, I was fortunate to make friends and became part of a group. One guy in our group, whom I still smile about today, was Jamaican. He was a great friend to us all and made us laugh so much with his comedic ways. His street dancing was hilarious and had us in stitches. We called him snowflake. He called us apple blossom. It wasn't considered offensive in any way and was just a bit of fun. I mention this only because it was so much a part of the times. Things have certainly changed. Also great excitement, the first local wine bar and coffee house opened up. We had somewhere to hang out which didn't cost a bomb. For the time being, I was settled and living a reasonably normal life. Of course, with no parental control,

I had more freedom than most girls of my age; however, due to my circumstances, I had grown up very quickly. I was never going to join a gypsy camp again or become a sunbeam, although I still had to clean my own shoes! Even in a crowded room, it is possible to feel lonely. I did sometimes but was now able to look forward to some kind of future.

So my life continued in my bedsit—sometimes sharing and sometimes alone. I was there because I didn't have a choice. Some I shared with just wanted the experience of being away from home. A few didn't like it or me and went home again.

Eventually, I had a lovely flatmate. We became good friends. She worked unsociable hours delivering new cars, so she was up and out very early in the morning. We got used to this arrangement, and I was pleased to be with someone who shared my sense of humour and, more importantly, the cost of our bedsit. We invested a fair amount of money in our gas fire to keep warm and would spend some evenings chatting and laughing.

Sometime later, with much persuasion, I went out with a boy from work. I didn't want any more than friendship. We went to the cinema together, and he asked me to his office Christmas party. I had never been to a party before and didn't have anything to wear, so I borrowed a pink blouse with frills down the front and a tartan pleated skirt from my flatmate, which I felt good in. I don't really know how it fitted me because she was shorter and bigger, but somehow it worked. At least I think it did.

I arrived at the party with my friend, he of course knew his work colleagues, so I was left to my own devices. I chatted with everyone, most of them I had already spoken to on the telephone, so it was nice to put a face to a name.

Little did I know this party would shape the next years of my life. I met my future husband. He was holding court at the head of the table as office manager, wearing a black-and-white checked suit with hair Brylcreemed, as it was the fashion then. I introduced myself, saying he looked like a bookie's runner. He said I looked like something out of St Trinian's, and somehow we had a connection. I found out he was separated from his wife, who had walked out on him for someone else. There were no children. He asked me out, and I said that when his divorce was noted in the local paper, I would then be happy to see him again. I would point out that all divorcees were listed at this time. Besides which, I had no desire to be hurt again. The men in my life hadn't looked too promising to date.

Not long after this, his decree absolute came through. We became a couple. It hadn't started too well because he didn't turn up for our first date. Part of me was relieved and part of me disappointed. However, when I took a call from him on the switchboard at work the next day, he explained about an accident that prevented him from coming for me. Of course, there were no mobile phones and, in some cases, no house phones then. I can say his name is Douglas, as none of his family survives. I was nineteen years old, and Douglas was thirty-two. We didn't start out as the greatest love affair, but somehow we were meant to be together. We were treated to the old mantra 'This won't last, given the age gap' by most who knew us. Well, they were wrong. As in most marriages, there were times when it nearly didn't, but we worked through our problems when they arose.

Doubts did creep in even though as I have said we were meant to be together. I still didn't know how I felt or what I wanted to do with my life. I recalled the early mistakes I made, walking away from what was really a settled time. I knew the right thing to do was to encompass what I had now. Besides which, I admired and respected Douglas, and surely, that is the basis for a good relationship. I was also accepted by his family. But still, indecision tugged at my brain. I had several conversations with myself, saying how lucky I was. At last I belonged somewhere and was loved for who I am. I didn't have to wait around for the next move or the next decision as to my future. It really was down to me. During this time, when things were looking more positive, I thought about my mother. Of course, my life would have been different if she were still alive, but I hoped she would be pleased with the way I had eventually turned my life around with the help of Douglas and my friends.

Of course, a lot of help and guidance from Barnardo's got me here. I didn't always listen, being obstinate and defiant, and as I have said, I went off the rails. But life turned out much better for me than I could have hoped.

Douglas and I went on to have over forty years together and were married for thirty-eight of those. We have two daughters and three grandchildren, whom I absolutely adore and am extremely proud of.

My best friend and soulmate died in 2002 at the age of seventy-two after a very long illness. He was very brave and uncomplaining. I definitely got the best end of the deal and will treasure his memory forever. He was a wonderful husband, father, and granddad. We all knew him as Mampy, which is the name his grandchildren gave him.

Very sadly, he didn't live to meet my new best friend. Remember the little girl born in that stark, bleak mother-and-baby home all those years ago? . . . .

JUST A FINAL NOTE

Thank you very much for purchasing and reading my book. The older we get, maybe the wiser we become. Well, for me, the little bit of wisdom I acquired told me that most of my care workers were spinsters and would probably never know the joy of becoming a mother. The idea to separate my daughter from me was done for practical and economical reasons. They thought or knew we both stood a better chance in life individually. It doesn't excuse the cruelty of it all. Were they under the impression we would have difficulty surviving together? Who knows? I see that now and have to realize they made informed decisions, and I would assume they thought they were doing everything in our best interests. Who knows how we would have got on? I will never know, but I would have given anything at the time for a chance to try.

This doesn't mean forgiveness; it means acceptance. I am an avid reader of all genres, and sometimes, having reached the last page of a novel, I have thought there are a few things I didn't fully understand or I would like to discuss with the author—for example, the reasoning behind their story, how they came up with their ideas (fiction), and generally talk about their work. I did once belong to a book club which enabled discussions on certain books we read as a group. This helped but did not give an opportunity to approach an author.

I understand we now have social media—Twitter, Facebook, etc. I do not subscribe to any of these and do not wish to. I realize millions use these portals and enjoy doing so; however, they are not for me.

For this reason, if anyone would like to contact me to give their critique, please feel free to do so by email: *jvoyzey@btinternet. com*. Praise or constructive criticism is most welcome. This is my first journey into the world of writing and publishing, and I feel I would like to continue; however, unless I have feedback for *Ice Cream on Thursdays*, I will not know how well or badly received my maiden effort is.

With thanks and kind regards,

Jeanette Voyzey

Jeanette Voyzey (nee Jackson-Smith) was born in Eastleigh in Hampshire towards the end of the Second World War during an air raid and has been dodging fallout ever since.

She met Douglas in 1963, and they married in Oxford in 1965. They have two daughters and three grandchildren.

Jeanette was widowed in 2002 and moved from Witney to Bampton in Oxfordshire, where she currently lives. Her career to date has been mostly in sales; however, having worked from the age of fourteen, Jeanette is currently taking a break from the workforce.

She has a keen interest in the arts and theatre and is also an avid reader of all genres.

Lightning Source UK Ltd.
Milton Keynes UK
UKOW04f0608120214

226315UK00001B/42/P

9 781493 140381